PROFILES · IN · MUSIC
Elvis

LIBRARY OF CONGRESS CATALOGING-IN-PUBLICATION DATA

Loewen, Nancy, 1964-
    Elvis / by Nancy Loewen.
      p. cm. -- (Profiles in music)
    Includes index.
    Summary: Examines the life and career of the influential rock and roll star, from his early years in Mississippi to his controversial death.
    ISBN 0-86592-606-9
    1. Presley, Elvis, 1935-1977--Juvenile literature. 2. Rock musicians--United States--Biography--Juvenile literature.
    [1. Presley, Elvis, 1935-1977. 2. Musicians. 3. Rock music.]
    I. Title. II. Series: Loewen, Nancy, 1964- Profiles in music.
ML3930.P73L6 1989
782.42166'092--dc20
[B]
[92]   89-32264
                                                                       CIP
                                                                     MN AC

© 1989 Rourke Enterprises, Inc.

All rights reserved. No part of this book may be reproduced or utilized in any form or by any means, electronic or mechanical, including photocopying, recording or by any information storage and retrieval system without permission in writing from the publisher.

PROFILES · IN · MUSIC
Elvis

**TEXT BY
NANCY LOEWEN**

**DESIGN & PRODUCTION BY
MARK E. AHLSTROM**
(The Bookworks)

**ROURKE
ENTERPRISES,
INC.**
Vero Beach, FL 32964
U.S.A.

ELVIS ARON PRESLEY
1935-1977

TABLE OF CONTENTS

Introduction	6
Chapter 1: From Tupelo to Memphis	13
Chapter 2: Elvis Takes Off	25
Chapter 3: Good Rockin' Tonight!	37
Chapter 4: Serving the Nation	63
Chapter 5: Still the King	75
Chapter 6: Elvis: Never Forgotten	93
Glossary	108-109
Index	110
Listening Choices	111

CREDITS

PHOTOS AND ILLUSTRATIONS

H. Gris/FPG .... cover photo, 4
Photoworld/FPG .... 12, 53, 58, ... 71, 106-107
FPG 46
Carson Baldwin, Jr./FPG 54
Travelpix/FPG 55
Leon Dishman/FPG 56-57
Peter Borsari/FPG 59, 61
Dwight Ellefson/FPG 60
Apger/FPG 62
Las Vegas News Bureau/FPG .92

TYPESETTING AND LAYOUT: THE FINAL WORD
PRINTING: WORZALLA PUBLISHING CO.

Elvis Presley: King of Rock 'n' Roll

As soon as Elvis Presley steps onstage, he is surrounded by light. Thousands of cameras flash. Hundreds of spotlights make his white, jewel-encrusted costume sparkle and shine. Behind him the words "We Love Elvis" flash in twelve languages.

It is January 1973, and this is no ordinary concert. As Elvis Presley performs at the Honolulu International Center in Hawaii, people from Australia, Japan, Korea, and other countries are gathered around their TV sets, watching the performance as it happens. The next night the show will be seen all across Europe. In April it will be shown in the United States.

Elvis Presley's "Aloha Satellite Show" will eventually be seen by one-and-one-half **billion** people. It is the most expensive entertainment special ever produced.

If Elvis Presley feels any stage fright, he certainly doesn't show it. The history-making singer looks fit and confident—"more handsome than ten movie stars," as one of his bodyguards put it. His voice is smooth and expressive. When he sings old favorites such as "Love Me Tender" and "Blue Suede Shoes," the live audience bursts into delighted applause.

During songs and between them, he leans into the front row of the audience. The eager fans kiss him and drape leis over his head. Some people hold out towels, which Elvis quickly touches to his face before returning. The towels, the handshakes, the kisses—all will be treasured by these devoted fans for years to come.

The concert is nearly over now. Elvis has sung more than 20 songs, and is now closing with "I Can't Help Falling in Love With You." As he finishes the song, he stands dramatically with his legs wide apart. His fist is in the air. His head is down. Slowly, he straightens up, flinging his jeweled cape into the frenzied crowd. The applause grows even louder as he spends a few more moments shaking the outstretched hands of his fans. Then he walks backstage, jumps into a limousine, and is whisked away into the night.

It has been one of Elvis Presley's most memorable performances.

• • •

Ask just about any established rock star to name someone who had an important influence on his or her music. From former Beatle Paul McCartney to Bruce Springsteen, the answer is the same: Elvis Presley.

With a sneer, a bump of his hips, and a driving beat, Elvis Presley shook up the musical scene in the 1950's. He was one of the first performers to successfully combine black rhythm & blues with white country music. The new sound—rock 'n' roll—was immediately accepted by teenagers as **their** music. No longer did they have to listen to the same music their parents did. This was a new generation!

But if Elvis Presley helped create a generation gap, he also helped close the gap between blacks and whites. At the time Elvis made it big, segregation was still common. Those attitudes extended to music, too. Much as they may have wanted to, whites just didn't listen to black musicians, and vice versa. Through his music, Elvis Presley helped bring people together. "Elvis was a blessing," said black rock 'n' roller Little Richard. "He opened the door for black music."

Elvis Presley was born in Tupelo, Mississippi, in 1935. His family was very poor. No one could have predicted the fame that awaited him. But by the time Elvis was 20 years old, he already had a devoted following. And by 1975, he had sold more than 500 million records.

That kind of success has its price. Elvis was often lonely and isolated. He spent his life running from private jet to private limousine, hardly ever seeing the light of day. Many of his closest friends were also on his payroll.

Elvis Presley died of a heart attack on August 16, 1977, at the age of 42. The impact on the nation was almost as if a president had died. Thousands of grieving fans quickly gathered around his Memphis mansion called Graceland. As far away as Japan, music critics openly sobbed on the radio as they discussed his contribution to the music industry and to the world.

Though many years have passed since Elvis' death, he has not been forgotten. In fact, many people refuse to believe he is dead. Some people say that Elvis faked his death in order to get away from the pressures of superstardom. One woman even wrote a book about this idea. The book comes with a cassette tape of what supposedly is Elvis' voice—"proving" that he is still alive! All across the country, there are reports of "Elvis sightings."

Elvis' family, too, continues to attract attention. His former wife, Priscilla Presley, is a successful actress. His daughter, Lisa Marie, married musician Danny Keough in 1988. When she turns 30 in 1998, Lisa will inherit her father's estate. By then, Elvis Presley's legacy to his daughter may be worth as much as $100 million.

People still buy Elvis Presley records. They rent his movies and listen to his songs on the radio. Mementos, from collector plates to bumper stickers saying "I ❤ Elvis," are still being snapped up. Graceland, open to the public since 1982, is one of the most-visited homes in the nation. More than a half million people visit Elvis' mansion each year!

Perhaps the most amazing aspect of Elvis' career is the incredible loyalty of his fans. For them, "the King" lives on.

By the time he was 21, Elvis had shaken up the world with a new kind of music—"rock 'n' roll."

CHAPTER 1: FROM TUPELO TO MEMPHIS

"Dad packed all our belongings and put them on the top and in the trunk of a 1939 Plymouth. We just headed to Memphis. Things had to get better."

—Elvis

Identical Twins

Elvis Presley may have died a millionaire, but he surely wasn't born one. His parents, Vernon and Gladys, were very poor. They lived in the small town of Tupelo, Mississippi. Vernon Presley held a number of jobs, including those of a truck driver and factory worker. Gladys was a sewing machine operator. She worked from six in the morning to six at night, five or six days a week. Even so, they were barely able to make a living.

When Vernon and Gladys were first married, they took turns living with their in-laws. Then Gladys became pregnant. With some help from one of Vernon's bosses, they managed to rent a house of their own in East Tupelo. The house had only two rooms. There was no running water. An outhouse stood in the backyard. Still, the Presleys were excited. They finally had a place of their own.

Soon Gladys had to quit her job, and money became even more scarce. Her pregnancy was very difficult, and she thought she knew the reason for it. "I'm carrying twins!" Gladys kept insisting to her doctor. But the doctor didn't believe her.

Finally, on January 8, 1935, she gave birth to a boy whom they named Elvis Aron. Then it turned out that her hunch was right. Elvis' identical twin brother, Jesse Garon, was born a short while later. Sadly, Jesse died almost right away. Placed in a tiny coffin, he was buried the next day in an unmarked grave in the nearby Priceville Cemetery.

Some people think that because Elvis had an identical twin, he had greater psychic powers than most people. But because his "other half" was dead, Elvis was also "incomplete." To the people who believe this way, the circumstances of his birth explain a great deal about the nature of Elvis Presley.

Early Lessons

Elvis' parents—especially Gladys—showered their young son with affection and love. They spoiled him as much as they could afford to. But they also were very strict when it came to things like good manners. As soon as he could talk, Elvis was taught to say "Ma'am" and "Sir" and to stand up when an older person entered the room. His parents also tried to teach him the values of honesty and fairness.

One time young Elvis found a Coke bottle on his neighbor's porch. For some reason, he decided that he wanted it. So, without asking, he picked it up and took it home with him.

"Did Mrs. Harris give you that?" Gladys asked when she saw him. "No," Elvis had to admit. Gladys gave him a spanking. "You didn't ask first!" she explained. Then she marched him back to Mrs. Harris' place to apologize for what he'd done. Mrs. Harris let him keep the bottle after all—and gave him cookies besides.

Just a block and a half away from their little house stood the First Assembly Church of God. The Presley family attended the services regularly. Sometimes, when Elvis was still very young, he would slip off his mother's lap and run down the aisle to the front of the church. Then he'd just stand there, looking at the choir and trying to sing with them. Years later, Gladys said proudly, "He was too little to know the words, of course, but he could carry the tune."

The gospel songs and spirituals Elvis sang in that little church would play an important part in his musical roots. Even some of his controversial stage moves were learned from revival ministers! As Elvis once explained, "We used to go to these religious singin's all the time. There were these singers, perfectly fine singers, but nobody responded to them. Then there was the preachers and they cut up all over the place, jumpin' on the piano, movin' ever which way. The audience liked 'em. I guess I learned from them."

By the time he was in the fifth grade, a few people had already discovered that Elvis had a talent for singing. One day he sang some songs in front of his class. His teacher was so impressed that she had him sing for the principal. Then the principal got excited, too. He entered Elvis in a singing contest at the Mississippi/Alabama State Fair. Standing on a chair in order to reach the microphone, Elvis sang a tune called "Old Shep." He won second place—and a prize of five dollars. Not only that, but he could get on all the rides for free, too. To a kid, the free rides probably meant more than the money!

In Exchange for a Bike

Before long, Elvis had his heart set on something most kids want: a bicycle. As always, Vernon and Gladys wanted to please their son. Vernon even shopped for the bike to see how much it would cost. But when he looked at the price tag, he had no choice but to say no. "I'm sorry, son," Vernon said firmly. "We just can't afford a bike right now." Elvis was very disappointed, but he knew his parents were right.

Then Gladys had an idea. "Elvis, how would you like a guitar instead? It could help you with your singing. And maybe you can get the bike later!" The guitar—in the same store window as the bike—cost about 13 dollars. Of course, Elvis still wanted the bike. But he agreed that if he got the guitar, he wouldn't say anything to his parents about the bike for another year.

Two of Elvis' uncles taught him a few chords on his new guitar. After he had learned to play a little, he would sit in front of the radio, guitar in hand. Then he tried to pick out the melodies he heard, or strum chords as an accompaniment.

Elvis listened to country singers like Roy Acuff and Jimmie Rodgers. He also liked the blues music of black musicians, including songs by B.B. King and Muddy Waters. Then there were the white spirituals he heard in church. Later, all of these influences would come together—and startle the world.

Moving to Memphis

In 1948, when Elvis was 13 years old, his family moved to Memphis, Tennessee. They were flat broke. "Dad packed all our belongings and put them on the top and in the trunk of a 1939 Plymouth. We just headed to Memphis," Elvis explained. "Things had to be better."

But it would be a long time before things improved.

The family moved into a one-room apartment in a bad neighborhood. There was no kitchen, so they had to cook over a hot plate—and hope the electric wiring didn't start a fire. There were holes in the walls, and during the winter the heating was terrible. They even had to share a bathroom with other families. The Presleys tried to make the best of it, though. This awful apartment was all they could afford.

In Memphis, Elvis attended L.C. Hume High School. The new school was a lot bigger than his old one, and at first Elvis was terrified. The first day of classes, Vernon walked him to school and came back home. A few minutes later, there at the door was Elvis! He was so scared the other kids would laugh at him that he refused to go back. But he agreed to go back the next day. In time, he slowly got used to his new school.

During this time, Elvis' parents took jobs wherever they could find them. Vernon worked at a tool company and drove a truck. Gladys sometimes worked in a curtain factory, or as a waitress. No matter how hard they worked, though, they still weren't getting ahead. After they'd been in Memphis for a year, they moved into a federal housing project at Lauderdale Courts. They now had two bedrooms and a nicer place, but the neighborhood was still bad. Gladys often worried about her only child.

Hidden Talents

At school, Elvis was not someone who got a lot of attention. He was an average student. His classmates later described him as friendly, polite, and a little shy. Sometimes he would play the guitar and sing for his friends, but only if they asked him to do it.

Elvis liked to hang out on Beale Street. That street was famous for all the talented black musicians who performed there, mostly in bars. Beale Street was known as "the home of the blues." Whenever Elvis had a little money, he spent it at a clothing store on Beale Street that sold all sorts of bright, unusual clothes. He especially liked the colors pink and black. Sometimes he wore a pink jacket with tight black pants. The next day he might wear a black jacket with pink pants.

If Elvis Presley stood out for anything in high school, it was for his unusual clothes and his long hair. At that time, just about all the men and boys wore their hair in crew cuts. Not Elvis. He liked wearing his hair longer, in a "ducktail." He had long sideburns, too. He was always combing his hair, and he didn't care who saw him.

Some of his classmates didn't care much for a

guy who paid that much attention to his hair. "I remember once when all the guys were gonna get him and cut his hair," said Red West, one of Elvis' high school friends who later became his bodyguard. "I helped him escape from that."

When Elvis was a junior in high school, he made the football team as an end—even though he was smaller than most of his teammates. He mainly played defense, and never scored any touchdowns for Hume High School. During his senior year, he had a fight with his coach about his long hair. "You either cut your hair, or you get off the team," the coach said sternly. Elvis quit the team.

Every year, Hume High School put on a variety show to raise money for a special school fund. There were a lot of poor students in the school. If someone couldn't afford to go to a dance, or needed money for lunches or decent clothes, they could talk to the principal. Without anyone else knowing about it, they could get money from this fund.

Elvis' homeroom teacher, Miss Scrivener,

wanted him to sing at the show. At first he didn't want to do it. The idea of him getting up there in front of all his classmates—and teachers—was terrifying! Somehow Miss Scrivener managed to talk him into it. Maybe it was because he realized he would be helping other poor kids, like himself.

Elvis was very nervous before going onstage. Once he started singing, though, he was fine. The first song he sang was a love song. Elvis sang it with such emotion that some of the teachers started to cry! Then he sang some faster songs. His classmates couldn't believe it. Was this really the shy Elvis Presley they knew?

In the variety show, the winner was the student who got the most applause. That person could do an encore. "It's you, Elvis," Miss Scrivener whispered to him backstage, nudging him to go on again. When he finished the encore, he was all smiles. "They liked me, they really liked me!" he exclaimed in surprise to his teacher.

CHAPTER 2: ELVIS TAKES OFF

"Only blacks have any freshness to their music these days. If I could just find a white man who sounded black, I could make a billion dollars."

—Sam Phillips, Sun Records

A Special Birthday Present

The financial situation of the Presley family was getting more complicated. At one point, when they thought they wouldn't be able to make it, Gladys went to work as a nurses' aid in a hospital. Then the housing authorities threatened to evict them—because their income was too high for them to remain in the project!

Finally, in 1953, they moved into a small apartment near the center of Memphis. That June, Elvis graduated from high school. His diploma became one of his most prized possessions, even when he had reached the peak of his musical success. He was the first member of the Presley family to graduate from high school.

Now that he was done with school, it was time for Elvis to go to work. He was soon hired by Crown Electric Company as a truck driver. This suited Elvis just fine. He drove all over Memphis and the surrounding area, making deliveries and picking up supplies. His salary was $1.25 an hour.

Elvis was Crown's youngest employee, and his co-workers thought it was fun to tease him and play tricks on him. They liked him, though—even though they just couldn't understand his long hair!

Elvis was happy driving a truck. Having a steady job was very important to him. When he turned over most of his wages to his mother, he felt very proud. Being able to help out his family meant a lot to him.

On one of his runs, Elvis passed by the Memphis Recording Service. This was a sideline business of the Sun Record Company, owned by Sam Phillips. The service recorded special events, such as weddings. The most popular service they offered, though, was to let people make their own records. It cost four dollars to record two songs directly onto a small record.

This gave Elvis an idea. His mother's birthday was coming up. Wouldn't she just love a record made by her own son! Elvis started to save his money for the project. One Saturday afternoon during his lunch break, he parked Crown's Ford pickup in the parking lot of the Memphis Recording Service and went inside.

Elvis was met by a woman named Marion Keisker, a former radio personality who helped run the office. She liked to keep an eye out for people with special talent. Making conversation as Elvis waited his turn in line, Marion Keisker asked him what famous singer he sounded like. "I don't sound like nobody," Elvis replied.

Marion raised an eyebrow. That's what they all say, she thought to herself. But when it was Elvis' turn to record, she listened carefully.

As Marion listened to Elvis, she remembered something she'd often heard Sam Phillips say. "Only the blacks have any freshness in their music these days," he'd sigh. "If I could just find a white man who sounded black, I could make a billion dollars." Marion thought Elvis might just be that person. Hurriedly she turned on a tape recorder, so Sam could hear him, too. Before Elvis left that day, she took down his name and address.

Elvis sang "My Happiness" and "That's When Your Heartaches Begin." He accompanied himself on the old guitar he'd gotten long ago, when his family was too poor to afford a bicycle.

Sam Phillips liked the tape. But he wasn't ready to do anything about it. "This Elvis still needs a lot of work," he said, and seemed to forget all about the young singer.

"That's All Right, Mama"

Marion didn't forget about Elvis, however. Eight months later, Sam needed someone to record a new song he'd just received. "How about trying the kid with the sideburns?" Marion suggested. When Sam agreed, Marion got on the phone. Getting in touch with Elvis wasn't easy. She had to call the Presley's neighbors because the family still didn't have a telephone.

Elvis came to the studio as soon as he got the

news. He was panting so hard, Marion figured he must have run all the way! But when Elvis tried the new ballad, he was terrible. He wasn't right for the song at all. Everyone was disappointed, most of all Elvis.

Still, there must have been something about Elvis Presley that made Sam Phillips take notice. When Elvis mentioned something about needing a backup band, Sam said, "I'll see what I can do." Then he arranged for Elvis to practice with a guitarist named Scotty Moore and a bass player named Bill Black.

For months, the new group worked hard at their music. Nearly every night after work they met at the small Sun recording studio and rehearsed. Nothing was happening, though. At that point, Elvis wasn't singing like he wanted to. He was singing like he thought **they** wanted him to.

Then one day, during a break, Elvis picked up his guitar and just started clowning around. Jumping around the room, he sang "That's All Right, Mama," a song by black blues singer Arthur

Crudup. Scotty and Bill joined in the fun.

Suddenly Sam Phillips ran into the room. "What are you doing?" he cried. "That's it! Keep doing that and we'll put it on tape." The group managed to hold on to the unique sound. And as the tape was made, history was made as well.

Sam Phillips decided to release "That's All Right, Mama" as a single. Now all they needed was a song for the flip side. For the next several nights, Elvis and his backup band worked on a song called "Blue Moon of Kentucky." At last they got it right. Elvis Presley's first record was released in the summer of 1954.

When it came to promoting the record, Sam Phillips was at a loss. It didn't really fit into any existing category. Finally he took it to a DJ named Dewey Phillips. Though the two men had the same last name, they weren't related—that they knew of, anyway. Dewey had a show on Memphis radio station WHBQ. The show, called "Red Hot and Blue," featured work by black blues artists. Though Elvis was white, Dewey played the new record over and over on his program.

In a few days, Sun Records had orders for 5,000 records from music stores in the area.

"That's All Right, Mama" soon climbed to the number one spot on Memphis' country charts, even though it wasn't really "country." *Billboard*, a leading music magazine, took note of the unique style and praised Elvis' first record. But although the record sold well in the South, the rest of the country hardly noticed it.

Mixed Reviews

Before joining up with Elvis, Scotty Moore and Bill Black had a group called the Starlight Wranglers. After Elvis' record hit, though, the other band members felt left out. Soon they all quit. Rather than finding a new name for the threesome, Elvis simply became a part of the Starlight Wranglers. The success of "That's All Right, Mama" started bringing the Wranglers some small gigs.

The first time Elvis performed in front of a

large audience was at an all-country show at the Overton Park Shell in Memphis. He wasn't the featured performer. In fact, his name wasn't even on the posters. But when he sang "Good Rockin' Tonight" for the evening show, he put the crowd into a frenzy. They loved him!

"I came out on stage and I was scared stiff. My first big appearance in front of an audience," Elvis remembered later. "I came out and I was doin' a fast-type tune, and ever'body was hollerin' and I didn't know what they was hollerin' at. I came off stage and my manager told me they was hollerin' because I was wigglin'. Well, I went back out for an encore and I kinda did a little more. And the more I did, the wilder they went."

Juggling his job and his music soon got to be too much, so Elvis quit his truck-driving job at Crown. It was a smart decision. Sam Phillips, using all of his connections, managed to book Elvis and his band on two important country music radio programs, "Louisiana Hayride" and "Grand Ole Opry." Elvis was especially excited about appearing on "Opry," which was held at the Grand Ole Opry concert hall in Nashville. To most country performers, that was the peak of success. Getting booked onto the show so early in his career was quite a feat.

When the booking manager of the "Grand Ole Opry" saw Elvis with his two-member backup band, however, he had a fit. "You promised me it would be just like the record!" he exclaimed angrily. Apparently he thought it had taken many more players to come up with such a "big" sound.

The booking manager wasn't quite ready for Elvis' performing style, either. "You might consider driving a truck again," he said bluntly after the show. Elvis was so upset that he cried during most of the long drive home.

Luckily, Elvis' appearance on "Louisiana Hayride," held in Shreveport, Louisiana, went a lot better. In fact, he got the crowd so worked up that he was offered a year's contract to come on the show each week.

"There's Good Rockin' Tonight!"

In January 1955, Elvis' second single on the Sun label was released. It was the song that had gotten the crowd at Overton Park all excited, "Good Rockin' Tonight." Once again, *Billboard* paid attention to Elvis. The write-up said that he appealed not only to country fans but also to rhythm & blues and pop fans as well. In those days, very few performers managed to cross those boundaries. There was no doubt about it—Elvis Presley was someone special.

Soon it became obvious that he needed a manager to organize his appearances and handle the finances. He turned to Bob Neal, a famous disc jockey on WMPS in Memphis. The agreement was a simple one, but since Elvis was under 21, his parents had to give their approval.

Under Bob Neal's management, Elvis, Scotty, and Bill became the Blue Moon Boys. The "Louisiana Hayride" contract was extended. They also started doing three or four other concerts a week. Sometimes Bob himself would emcee the performance. His wife would sell tickets at the door.

Bob Neal soon had the Blue Moon Boys running from one gig to another. Besides appearing in Tennessee, they also covered Louisiana, Florida, Alabama, and Mississippi. Elvis was getting more and more popular, especially with teenage girls. He was tall, blue-eyed, and handsome—and even though his hair was really blonde, he put so much grease in it that it looked dark. Besides that, he had an easy, natural stage presence. When he looked over his audience, his gaze made them all feel he was looking at no one but them.

"You'd see this frenzied reaction, particularly from the young girls," Bob Neal once explained about those early days. "We hadn't gone out and arranged for anyone to squeal and scream...For Elvis they just did it automatically."

CHAPTER 3 — GOOD ROCKIN' TONIGHT!

"I don't know what happens to me when I sing. Maybe it's the music, the song, the crowd, or something deep inside me, but to the rock 'n' roll beat I have to move my hands, feet, knees, legs, my head—everything."

—Elvis

An Unbeatable Team

Elvis' third single, "Milkcow Blues Boogie," got hardly any attention at all. But things changed when his next record came out. "Baby, Let's Play House" made it not only on the local charts, but on the national charts as well! The single after that, "Mystery Train," also did well. Elvis was becoming popular all across the United States.

A lot of people in the entertainment business were keeping their eye on Elvis Presley. One of them was Colonel Tom Parker. In 1955, the stocky, cigar-smoking Parker was already a legend of sorts. He had managed two of country music's best acts, Hank Snow and Eddy Arnold. Now he began to take an interest in Elvis.

Colonel Tom Parker grew up in a traveling carnival. His motto was "Don't explain it, just sell it!" He was always coming up with clever promotional schemes. One time he was promoting a carnival that wasn't drawing many people.

Instead of lowering the admission price—which is what most people would have done—he doubled it. Then he guaranteed that if the people weren't satisfied, they'd get half their money back.

Of course, everyone wanted half their money back. But the crazy idea worked. Attendance zoomed up, and they hadn't lowered their price by one cent!

Besides being a shrewd promoter, Colonel Parker had the ability to recognize true talent when he saw it. And he saw lasting talent in Elvis. Soon after Bob Neal became Elvis' manager, Colonel Parker worked together with Neal to arrange some of Elvis' bookings. Colonel Parker spent a lot of time watching how audiences responded to Elvis. He liked what he saw.

Soon the Colonel decided that he wanted to become Elvis' permanent manager. That was fine with Bob Neal, who had many other projects as well and couldn't devote all of his time to Elvis Presley. Elvis didn't raise any objections to the prospect of a new manager. Now the only trick was to get Elvis' parents to agree with the plan.

Because Elvis was not yet 21, his parents would have to sign any legal documents for him.

Colonel Parker wasted no time. He called on Vernon and Gladys often, and soon convinced them that he had their son's best interests at heart. The documents were signed, and Colonel Parker became Elvis' new manager.

Around this time, Sam Phillips at Sun Records was considering selling Elvis' recording contract. The Colonel was a strong force in the negotiations, and a deal was struck with RCA/Victor Records in late summer of 1955.

Elvis' early days at Sun, however, would never be forgotten. In fact, Sam Phillips himself is considered an important influence on the music of that period. His small recording company helped launch the careers of such notable performers as Johnny Cash, Jerry Lee Lewis, Carl Perkins, and Roy Orbison.

A Better Roof Overhead

Now that he was signed with a bigger record company, Elvis was starting to earn a lot of money from the sales of his records. One of his favorite things to buy was cars, and like a lot of country singers, he went for Cadillacs. But he also bought something more permanent—a nice house. This was a dream come true for his whole family.

One of his former bosses at Crown, Mrs. Tipler, wasn't surprised when she found out about the house. "Before he ever knew he was going to make a nickel, one day he sat here in our office and said, 'If I ever get my hands on some money, I'm gonna buy my mother a home,'" she said.

The new house was on Audubon Drive, a wealthy area of Memphis. When the teenagers found out where Elvis was living, they swarmed the place. By 1956, Elvis had to build tall brick walls around the estate just to have a little privacy.

The neighbors in this rich community often complained about all the kids hanging around. Then they found something else to get upset about. Rumor had it that Gladys Presley herself still hung out her family's wash on a clothesline. "How tacky!" cried the snooty neighbors, most of whom had servants to take care of such jobs. None of this stopped Gladys from hanging her clothes out in the fresh air. And as it turned out, the Presleys were the only ones on the block to own their house outright. The others were still paying off their mortgages.

"Heartbreak Hotel"

A lot of famous people were paying attention to Elvis Presley by now. Not all of them had good things to say. Ed Sullivan was the host of a very popular television variety show. Many of his viewers were clamoring for Sullivan to invite Elvis as a guest on his show. But Sullivan wouldn't budge. "I wouldn't touch Elvis Presley with a ten-foot pole!" he insisted.

Fortunately, others were more willing to cash in on Elvis' popularity. Elvis made his first television appearance on January 28, 1956, on a CBS summer replacement show called "The Dorsey Brothers." The show was produced by Jackie Gleason. It was on at the same time as the "Perry Como Show," and was in desperate need of better ratings. Colonel Parker worked his magic on the deal. He got Elvis and his crew six appearances on the show—and a good sum of money besides.

January 28 was a cold, rainy night. Few people were in the New York studio audience— and some of those were only seeking shelter from the storm! Elvis knew he'd have to create a little storm himself, to get the audience excited about his music.

His first song was a new one, "Heartbreak Hotel." As he sang, Elvis Presley used every trick he knew of. He jerked his legs, thumped his guitar, bumped his hips, sneered, and smiled that crooked smile. When he looked into the camera with those heavy-lidded eyes, teenagers all across

America knew they had found a hero.

"Heartbreak Hotel" was released by RCA that same week. Just one week later, *Billboard* reported that record sales had "snowballed." Elvis was about to have his first number one record. It would stay in that position for eight weeks.

All during this time, though, Elvis and the others in the band hardly realized they had a hit. Colonel Parker had them on the road all the time. They were very busy—driving all night, sleeping during the day, playing their shows and then rushing off to their next date. They hardly even saw the newspapers. The late-night radio they listened to while driving didn't tell them very much. True, the crowds they played to went crazy for Elvis. But they'd been doing that for a long time already!

The Real Presley

Other television appearances soon followed. In March 1956, and again in June, Elvis appeared on the "Milton Berle" show. All across the country, families started arguing about him. Elvis' wild stage movements were upsetting to many of the adults. Parents thought he was disgraceful. Television critics actually called him a threat to society!

The kids, on the other hand, thought he was the best thing that ever happened.

That July, Elvis made an appearance on the "Steve Allen Show." He sang "Hound Dog," the song that would be his next release. But it wasn't a typical performance. Elvis was asked to sing to a real dog that was trained to just sit there, looking droopy. Elvis was also asked to stand perfectly still, so as not to offend the television audience.

Elvis disliked the arrangement almost as much as his new nicknames: "Elvis the Pelvis" and "Swivel Hips." But he didn't want to make a big fuss. He did as he was told.

Many of Elvis Presley's fans were upset when they saw the show. The very next day, some of them picketed the studio theater. "We want the

One of Elvis' most famous songs, "Hound Dog," was first sung on the "Steve Allen Show" in 1956—to a real hound.

real Presley!" their signs proclaimed.

The storm really hit when Elvis Presley made an appearance on the "Ed Sullivan Show" on September 9, 1956. By now, Elvis had become too important to ignore. Sullivan finally had to admit that he was wrong about not inviting him to appear on the show. But that's not all. With Colonel Parker handling the negotiations, Sullivan had to pay $15,000 for one appearance. That was three times what other top performers were paid!

While Sullivan agreed to that outrageous price, he really wasn't too happy about having Elvis on the show. Just to be on the safe side, he made sure the cameras only shot Elvis from the waist up. But the screams from the studio audience told the whole story.

That night, Sullivan's show got a record-setting 82.6 percent of the television audience—or 54 million people! This record stood until 1964, when a British band called the Beatles made their first appearance on U.S. television, also on the "Ed Sullivan Show."

That Rock 'n' Roll Beat

Within a week of Elvis' first appearance on the "Ed Sullivan Show," RCA released seven new Elvis Presley singles all at once. This was a risky move. Critics of the idea thought that the songs would compete with one another. But it soon became obvious that Elvis was no ordinary recording star.

RCA's plan worked. "Hound Dog" quickly made number one. "Don't Be Cruel" and "Love Me Tender" followed suit. From August to December 1956, Elvis Presley was the only artist in the top position. In a way the songs did compete with one another—for being number one!

Whether the public liked Elvis or hated him, just about everyone had something to say on the subject.

"I'm in **love** with Elvis Presley!" sighed teenage girls as they rushed to buy Elvis' latest records. "He's an OK sort of guy," said the boys as they started growing out their hair in order to look more like Elvis.

Parents were horrified. "Elvis Presley is trash—an absolute disgrace!" they complained at supper tables across the nation. "Go spend your allowance on something worthwhile!" But the more the adults protested, the faster their kids bought Elvis' records.

The commotion over Elvis Presley just got bigger. In Michigan, a teenage boy was kicked out of school for refusing to cut his ducktail and sideburns. In New York, a group of women circulated a petition asking that Elvis be banned from television. In Canada, eight students were expelled from the Notre Dame Convent just for going to one of his concerts!

Elvis wasn't upset by all the fuss, but he was a little surprised. "I don't know what happens to me when I sing," he admitted once. "Maybe it's the music, the song, the crowd, or something deep inside me, but to the rock 'n' roll beat I have to move my hands, feet, knees, legs, my head—everything."

Despite all the criticism, Elvis didn't change his style of performing. Later on, he explained, "I watch my audience and listen to them, and I know that we're all getting something out of our system and none of us knows what it is. The important thing is we're getting rid of it and nobody's getting hurt."

It was an idea that few adults were able to understand at that time.

Hollywood Debut

Of course, Colonel Parker wasn't one to sit idly by while there was money to be made. He made sure the demand for Elvis Presley went farther than records and performances. He oversaw the production of all kinds of special Elvis products. Teenagers couldn't get enough of Elvis Presley bobby socks, shoes, clothes, pajamas, jewelry, handkerchiefs, bubble gum cards, diaries, pens, pencils, and other items. There was even an Elvis Presley picture that glowed in the dark!

As profitable as all of that was, the Colonel had his sights set on something even bigger—Hollywood. Colonel Parker got Elvis a part in a new movie. It was a love story set during the Civil War, and was originally called *The Reno Brothers*. When Elvis joined the cast, though, four songs were added and the title was changed to *Love Me Tender*.

At first, Hollywood actors were leery of Elvis. What did he know about acting? They soon discovered that Elvis was very easy to work with. Even though he wasn't the star of the movie, he worked hard. He had no problem learning his lines—and everyone else's, for that matter. He was always very polite. In fact, sometimes he was **too** polite.

In one scene, actress Mildred Dunnock ordered him to drop his gun. Elvis was supposed to refuse. But the scene had to be redone several times because Elvis would automatically drop the gun! "You could see he was used to obeying older people, especially his mother," commented Mildred Dunnock to *Newsweek* in 1977. "It was a touching thing."

In November 1956, Elvis' first movie was released. *Love Me Tender* was an enormous box-office hit. Never before had a movie made a profit so quickly! Although the critics panned the film and Elvis' performance, his fans didn't really notice or care. They just wanted the chance to see Elvis. In New Orleans, a girl sat through the movie 42 times. She even went to the previous movie 42 times—just so she could see Elvis in the previews!

Elvis continued to work in Hollywood, and the following summer, his second movie was released. This time he was the star. The movie was called *Loving You*, and told the rags-to-riches story of a small-town orphan. Of course, Elvis played the part of the orphan. In October, another Elvis movie—*Jailhouse Rock*—came out. Elvis might not have won over the hearts of the critics, but the hearts of the teenagers were all his. Both movies were big hits.

Elvis performed in his hometown of Tupelo, Mississippi, shortly before the release of his first movie.

Even before he made it big, Elvis dreamed of buying a nice home for his family. Shown above is Graceland, which Elvis bought in 1957.

Graceland has been open to the public since 1982. Each year, thousands of fans come to Memphis to visit the home of their late hero.

"All I want is to be treated as a regular G.I.," Elvis said when he was drafted into the army. Here Elvis is shown relaxing with his fellow recruits.

Altogether, Elvis made more than 30 movies during his Hollywood career.

When Elvis made his comeback in 1968, it had been many years since he'd performed in front of live audiences. He was nervous at first—but his fans were eager to welcome him back.

Elvis' "Aloha Satellite Show" was one of his most memorable performances. The show was broadcast around the world.

Priscilla Beaulieu was just 14 years old when she first met Elvis Presley. She married him in 1967, at the age of 21.

Elvis was "discovered" in 1954 by Sun Records in Memphis. Within two years, he had become a worldwide sensation.

CHAPTER 4
SERVING THE NATION

"All I want is to be treated as a regular G.I. I want to do my duty and I'm mighty proud to be given the opportunity to serve my country."

—Elvis

You're In the Army Now!

Besides making movies, Elvis spent part of 1957 supervising the remodeling of the new house he'd bought in March. Actually, it was more than a house. It was really a mansion—with lots of spacious rooms, colonial pillars, and many acres of landscaped grounds. Elvis called it Graceland.

The Presleys' new home was located in Whitehaven, a small town that later became part of Memphis. At that time, the area surrounding Graceland wasn't developed. There weren't any neighbors living nearby, except for some cows in the pastures. And the cows pretty much left Elvis alone!

A ten-foot-high wrought iron gate stood at the entrance to the grounds. That's where the fans hung out, hoping for a glimpse of Elvis or maybe even an autograph. Whenever there was a report of a missing teenage girl, the very first thing the police did was check the crowd of girls around that gate!

Soon his fans had something other than Elvis' songs and movies to get worked up about. On January 20, 1958, Elvis Presley received orders to report to the Memphis Draft Board Office. He'd been drafted into the United States Army.

Elvis probably could have served in the army as an entertainer, like some other famous young performers had done. But he didn't want to go that route. "All I want is to be treated as a regular G.I.," he told reporters. "I want to do my duty and I'm mighty proud to be given the opportunity to serve my country."

Hollywood wasn't very pleased. Elvis' next movie, *King Creole*, was scheduled to start shooting the same week he was to report to basic training. Paramount had already put many thousands of dollars into the film. After writing the draft board a letter that explained the situation, Elvis managed to get a 60-day delay.

Like everything else in Presley's life, this delay caused a ruckus, too. Some people thought

Elvis' deferment was unfair to all the other recruits who didn't have his fame and fortune. Others thought Elvis shouldn't be drafted at all. They wondered what the enemy might do with him in a war situation. Then there were those whose main interest was whether or not Elvis Presley would have to get the regulation crew cut. (He did, by the way.)

Despite all the fuss, a lot of adults were happy about the situation. For two whole years, there would be no Elvis Presley shaking around on stage. And maybe by the time Elvis got out of the army, teenagers would have forgotten him.

It was wishful thinking.

A Death in the Family

After the filming for *King Creole* was completed, Elvis went to basic training at Ford Hood, Texas. He finished basic in late May of 1958—about the same time *King Creole* appeared at movie theaters. Unlike his other films, the critics really seemed to like this one. "Maybe Elvis really **can** act!" they said in surprise. Elvis was in great spirits.

Then something happened that made his career seem unimportant. In August, Elvis' mother became very ill with hepatitis. Her condition weakened, and on August 14, 1958, Gladys Presley died. The official cause of death was a heart attack.

Vernon and Elvis were devastated by Gladys' death. Their feelings about her were made evident by a marker placed a few feet in front of her 10-foot monument in the Forest Hill Cemetery in Memphis. "She was the sunshine of our home," the marker read.

It took a long time for Elvis to get over the death of his beloved mother. "I was an only child," said Elvis when he finally talked about it with reporters. "She was very close, more than a mother. She was a friend who would let me talk to her any hour of the day or night if I had a problem."

Soon afterwards, Elvis received orders to go

to an army base in Bremerhaven, Germany. With him went his father and grandmother. Elvis wanted to keep his remaining family close to him.

Out of Sight— But Not Out of Mind

In the army, Elvis' official job was to drive a jeep. His tour of duty was as normal as could be expected, considering his tremendous fame. His peers soon realized that Elvis just wanted to be "one of the guys." They teased him sometimes, but they respected him, too. Elvis' sergeant once defended him to the press, saying that Elvis "scrubbed, washed, greased, painted, marched, ran, carried his laundry, and worried through inspections just as everyone else did."

Still, there were a few things about his enlistment period that were different from most. He lived off-post in a house he rented with his father and grandmother. This went right along with army policy, though, since his family depended on Elvis for their support. Other soldiers had the same privilege. And for Elvis, "mail call" took on a whole new meaning. Most guys would be happy to get a few letters from home each week. Elvis usually got about 10,000!

Busy as he was, Elvis always managed to find time for two things: karate and dating. While in Germany, he earned his second-degree black belt. Karate would remain one of his hobbies for the rest of his life. In Germany he also met his future wife. Priscilla Beaulieu, then just 14 years old, was the daughter of an American Air Force captain stationed nearby. Although Presley dated lots of other girls, too, it was Priscilla who stayed on his mind.

While Elvis was in the army, a lot was happening in the lives of other popular musicians. Jerry Lee Lewis had been criticized by the public for marrying his 13-year-old cousin. Little Richard had given up rock music for the seminary. And Buddy Holly, Ritchie Valens, and the Big Bopper were all killed in a plane crash. These musicians and others had contributed a great deal to the music world. Yet it was Elvis who, despite his absence, remained the King of Rock 'n' Roll.

Elvis' army service hadn't harmed his career at all. In fact, it couldn't have worked out better. Elvis' absence made millions of hearts grow fonder. Not only did the kids still play his records, but also the parents stopped seeing him as such a threat. After all, Elvis was patriotic and had obviously loved his mother. How bad could he be?

Elvis is Back!

Sergeant Elvis Presley was discharged from the United States Army in March 1960 with a nearly perfect record. One of the first projects he undertook was a television special with Frank Sinatra. He also quickly released a new album, *Elvis is Back*. Then it was off to Hollywood to film his next movie, *G. I. Blues*.

It seemed that Elvis Presley was ready to pick

After nearly two years out of the limelight, Sergeant Elvis Presley faced a hungry press.

up where he had left off, much to the delight of his many fans.

There were some changes the second time around, though. Elvis had toned down his behavior as a performer. He sang more ballads. And he recorded an album of what had always been his favorite music: hymns and church songs. *His Hand in Mine* sold well, but it wasn't a big hit. Years later, however, his *Peace in the Valley* album would win Elvis his only Grammy award.

Changes were happening in his personal life as well. That summer, his father had remarried. And Elvis himself just couldn't forget about Priscilla Beaulieu. That holiday season of 1960, he flew her to Memphis for a visit. Because she was so young, he had to do a lot of talking to calm the fears of her parents. Finally, though, they agreed to let her come to Memphis.

The visit convinced both Elvis and Priscilla that they wanted to be together. After Priscilla returned home, Elvis got on the phone to the Beaulieus. He convinced Vernon and his new wife, Dee, to talk to the Beaulieus, too. Finally Priscilla's parents wore down. They agreed that she could come back to Memphis. Living with Elvis' family, Priscilla finished high school in Memphis.

In 1961, Elvis made what turned out to be his

last public appearance until 1968. He gave a benefit concert in Hawaii to raise money for the Memorial Fund of the USS *Arizona*. The *Arizona* was a battleship that had been sunk by Japanese divebombers during World War II. The benefit was given in the Block Arena in Pearl Harbor. Elvis sang 19 songs—probably his longest concert up to that point.

Other performers were involved with the show, too. They gained a new understanding of what it was like to live with Elvis' tremendous fame. For instance, as the entertainers tried to make their way from their taxi into the hotel where they were staying, the mob of Elvis fans pressed dangerously in on them. "I felt so close to death," country comedian Minnie Pearl related. "Everyone wants to be number one, but that experience was enough to convince me I don't want it."

A little while later, another experience made her feel the same way. After the benefit, Elvis stayed on to film his next movie, *Blue Hawaii*. Some of the other performers stayed on, too, just to have a good time. But Elvis' stardom had made ordinary pleasures impossible.

"They say he came down in the middle of the night to swim," remembered Minnie Pearl. "He couldn't come down during the day. He had the penthouse suite on top. We'd get out and act crazy, having the best time in the world. And we'd look up there and Elvis would be standing at the window, looking down at us."

CHAPTER 5 STILL THE KING

"You were our inspiration."

—the Beatles to Elvis

Good Ol' Boys

Elvis may have been lonely sometimes, but he was rarely alone. He was always surrounded by a group of men about his own age. These men were on his payroll. They did lots of things for Elvis, from being his bodyguards to keeping his wardrobe in shape. Their most important function, though, was to keep Elvis company. The press dubbed them the "Memphis Mafia" because most of them were from Memphis, too.

The Memphis Mafia kept a close watch on Elvis. If he seemed even a little bit tense, they knew it was time to horse around a little, have some fun. They played football and rode horses, watched movies, and listened to popular music. One of their favorite things to do at Graceland was to fill the swimming pool with flash bulbs and then shoot at them. The small explosions were exciting to see against a night sky. Even though it would take hours to clean the pool afterwards, no one complained.

When Elvis was in Memphis, he would sometimes rent a local amusement park for the night, after the park's normal hours. Then he and Priscilla—together with the Memphis Mafia and their wives or girlfriends—gaily went on one ride after another. The roller coaster was one of Elvis' favorites. Sometimes he even rode standing up—in the front car!

More and more often, though, the good times were mixed in with the bad. There was a lot of pressure on Elvis Presley, and he could get very moody. He worried a lot about his weight. Watching himself in his movies, he'd often mutter to himself, "No...too fat, too fat." For someone who loved to eat burnt bacon by the pound, though, staying in shape was a tough thing to do.

Elvis also had a temper. If he saw something on television that he didn't like, he sometimes picked up a gun and shot out the screen! And once, in a rage, he fired every single member of the Memphis Mafia and sent them packing. The next day, however, he settled down and gave them their jobs back.

But if the King got testy sometimes, he could also be very loyal and generous. Stories abound of Elvis giving away Cadillacs or expensive jewelry like they were candy. The Memphis car dealers would gladly open their doors at 3:00 a.m. if Elvis wanted to do some car shopping!

Elvis was also generous in other ways. When he heard that a boy who was dying of cancer wanted to meet him, Elvis was determined to make the boy's wish come true. He flew to Florida to visit the boy, and later gave him some autographed albums.

Alan Fortas, who was part of the Memphis Mafia, remembers another time when Elvis was especially caring. When Fortas' father was very ill, Elvis insisted that Fortas go to his father—yet stay on the payroll as well. "You stay in Memphis and if it's two years, you pick up your paycheck every week; and if you come back, you're fired," Elvis told him firmly. That Christmas, Elvis visited Fortas' father in the hospital and gave him a gold pocket watch.

Making Movies

Since being discharged from the army, Elvis Presley's career had taken a different turn. Gone were the days of television appearances and interviews. Gone were the days of the live concerts in front of frenzied crowds. For about nine years, Elvis did little but make movies and sound track albums. He was averaging three movies—and albums—a year!

Although Elvis Presley would never be taken very seriously as an actor, there was one thing the movie studios could count on. An Elvis Presley movie would turn a big profit. "They don't need titles," an MGM executive once remarked. "They could be numbered. They would still sell."

Thanks to Colonel Parker, Elvis himself was making an enormous amount of money from the movies. Besides getting paid $1 million a picture, he got a hefty percentage of the profits, too. After a while, though, even the money couldn't get him excited about what he was doing.

As more movies were made, the quality kept getting worse. The movie studio executives knew they could get by with a lot. An Elvis Presley picture would make a profit no matter how poorly it was made. And to make that profit even bigger, less and less time was spent in rehearsals.

This situation really bothered Elvis. Once, after finishing a film, He told the director, "Hey, there were some pretty funny things in the script." Then, without smiling, he added, "I'm gonna have to read it someday."

As much as he disliked what he was doing, Elvis couldn't seem to break out of the rut he was in. "Why is he doing this?" wondered his fans and critics alike. "He's wasting his talent!" A lot of people wanted to see him try more challenging roles. Others wanted him to forget the movies and get back to real rock 'n' roll.

Part of Elvis' problem may have been his reluctance to disagree with the Colonel. After all, his movies and records were making a fortune. Another reason may have been more personal. After making so many bad movies, Elvis was losing his confidence.

"I'm smart enough to realize that you can't bite off more than you can chew in this racket. You can't go beyond your limitations," Elvis Presley told reporters as early as 1963. "They want me to try an artistic picture. That's fine. Maybe I can pull it off someday. But not now...

"A certain type of audience likes me," he added. "I entertain them with what I'm doing. I'd be a fool to tamper with that kind of success."

Even if some were disappointed by the path Elvis was following, no one could deny his contribution to the music scene. Rock 'n' roll had become a permanent part of American and world culture, and Elvis Presley was still the King.

No one knew this better than another musical phenomenon—the Beatles. By 1965 the popular British group had become a worldwide sensation, but they hadn't forgotten their musical roots. Once, during a tour in California, they made it a point to stop by Elvis' Hollywood home. "You were our inspiration," they told the 30-year-old Elvis.

New Commitments

No matter what Elvis was doing, his name was often found in the headlines of the fan magazines and supermarket tabloids. One topic that got a lot of attention was Elvis Presley's love life. Whether Elvis dated up-and-coming actresses or "unknowns," someone was sure to write about it.

During all of this, Priscilla Beaulieu remained an important part of Elvis' life. Priscilla had graduated from high school in 1963, and had then gone to a finishing school in Memphis. She was still living at Graceland with Elvis' aunt and grandmother, or with Vernon Presley and his wife, Dee. One fan magazine speculated that Priscilla and Elvis were already married. Others laughed it off. "Elvis is having too much fun as a bachelor!" they insisted.

But on the morning of May 1, 1967, Elvis and Priscilla surprised everyone. They were married in a small, quick ceremony in Las Vegas. Following their "I do's" was a celebration breakfast for about 100 people. Wedding cake—all five feet of it—was included in the menu.

Now that Elvis wasn't a bachelor anymore, there were a few tensions among the Memphis Mafia. To begin with, a few of them didn't get along very well with Priscilla. They resented her influence on Elvis. To top that off, only two of them had been invited to the wedding. The others felt left out.

Except for Joe Esposito and Richard Davis, the rest of the Memphis Mafia left Elvis soon after the wedding. Their Hollywood connections soon got some of them jobs as stuntmen or extras. Others went back to Memphis and started their own careers in the recording industry. Eventually, though, many of them came back to work for Elvis.

Soon there was another "newcomer" to deal with. On February 1, 1968, Elvis and Priscilla's only child was born. They named their new daughter Lisa Marie. As soon as the word got out, Graceland was filled with booties, blankets, and toys sent by well-wishing fans. The hospital switchboard was lit up with calls from all over the world. It seemed like **everyone** wanted to say "congratulations."

Comeback!

Fatherhood must have agreed with Elvis. The same year his daughter was born, Elvis began breaking away from his movie rut. His comeback started with the enormous success of his hour-long Christmas television special on NBC.

The special was produced and directed by a man named Steve Binder. Binder knew how important the new project was to Elvis' career. "If Elvis did another 'MGM movie' on the special, he would wipe out his career. And he would be known only as that phenomenon who came along in the fifties, shook his hips and had a great manager," Binder said in Jerry Hopkins' *Elvis: A Biography*. "On the reverse side, if he could do a special and prove he was still number one, he could have a whole rejuvenation thing going."

The show was to be videotaped before a live audience in June. Elvis would be joined by all sorts of backup singers, instrumentalists, and dancers. In one number, his name would be spelled out in lights—twenty feet high!

The day of the taping, Elvis was all nerves. "I haven't been in front of those people in eight years!" he suddenly blurted out. "What am I gonna do if they don't like me? What if they laugh at me?" It was almost as if he was back at Hume High School, waiting to sing a few songs at the school variety show.

Then it was time to start the taping. He made his entrance wearing a black leather suit, looking as trim and handsome as ever. His hand shook as he reached for the microphone. Once he started singing, though, nothing could stop him.

As Elvis Presley sang the old hits, all the years melted away. In between songs he told stories and joked with the other performers. For a closing number, he sang a new song called "If I Can Dream." It had been written especially for the show. The single later sold more than one million copies.

The Christmas special was televised on NBC on December 3, 1968. That same week, RCA released the sound track of the special. Both proved that the King was back. As Jon Landau wrote in *Eye* magazine, "There's something magical about watching a man who has lost himself find his way back home."

Later, talking with Steve Binder, Elvis said, "I'm going to do things now."

That's the Way It Is

As good as 1968 had been, Elvis was determined to do even better in 1969. In January he booked 10 days with the American Recording Service in Memphis, which was headed by Chips Moman. The American Recording Service had a good in-house backup band. Elvis Presley liked the sound that came out of that studio. He wanted to be a part of it, too.

Although Elvis lost four days of the session because of laryngitis, he still wound up with his most productive recording session ever. He cut 36 songs in six days—more than enough for two albums. *From Elvis in Memphis* was released in May, and *Memphis/Vegas* was released later in the year.

Now that Elvis' movie days were over, the Colonel set his sights on another idea that would keep the money pouring in—Las Vegas concerts. The Hilton International Hotel opened in Las Vegas during the summer of 1969. At that time, it was the largest hotel there. Besides that, it had the world's largest casino. And the showroom was so big that not even Barbra Streisand could keep it filled during the hotel's grand opening.

"ELVIS" was the name people wanted to see on the enormous billboard outside the hotel. As soon as Elvis' appearance was announced, calls for reservations came in from all over the world.

As he was for his television special, Elvis was plenty nervous about the first Las Vegas show. "I'm just not sure I can cut it anymore," he told friends. But he rose to the challenge, putting together a tight show that included two backup singing groups (the Imperials and the Sweet Inspirations), band leader James Burton, and a host of talented instrumentalists. In the meantime, he also dieted and worked out. By the time of his engagement, Elvis was in prime form.

On opening night, Elvis stepped onstage. He braced his legs and snapped his knees, a pose from the 1950's. He opened his mouth to sing—and before he could get one word out, the crowd exploded. They clapped, screamed, shouted, stamped their feet, jumped up and down, whistled, and stood on their chairs. Elvis was back where he belonged.

That night, Elvis Presley's performance was every bit equal to the audience's welcome. And it didn't end there. For the entire month, Elvis gave two sell-out shows a day, seven days a week. Even the critics couldn't say enough about him. "Elvis was his own resurrection," said one writer in *Rolling Stone*.

Elvis Presley was on a roll now. One of his

new songs, "Suspicious Minds," went to number one on the charts. It had been seven years since an Elvis Presley song had reached the top spot! In January 1970, he had another month-long engagement in Las Vegas. Later in that year, he released a new album, *On Stage*. He also performed in the Astrodome in Houston.

In August, he went back to the Hilton International for his third engagement there. This time there were all sorts of camera crews following the action. MGM was making a documentary of Elvis' life, called *Elvis: That's the Way It Is*. The film was released in November to glowing reviews.

Just a few years earlier, there might not have been much interest in such a film. These days, however, Elvis Presley had proved once more that he was **still** the King.

"Don't Be Cruel"

Soon after Elvis finished his third Las Vegas engagement, he was off on his first tour since his comeback. Six concerts were given in six cities—Phoenix, St. Louis, Detroit, Miami, Tampa, and Mobile. In every city, tickets were sold out within hours of going on sale.

After taking a break for a couple of months, Elvis toured again. This time he mainly covered the West Coast. Then, in January 1971, he had another long engagement in Las Vegas. Wherever he went, Elvis Presley always drew a crowd.

That kind of fame also brought with it a problem: threats on Elvis' life. Throughout the years there had been many. Most of them weren't taken too seriously. There were a lot of disturbed people who got a kick out of making such threats. But that January in Las Vegas, Elvis had the scare of his life.

It began with a phone call. "There's a madman who's planning to kill Elvis during a show," a man said in a strange voice. "Give me $50,000 in unmarked bills and I'll tell you his name."

A few hours later, a menu from the hotel showroom was found in Elvis' message slot. Beside Elvis' picture on the menu, a gun had been drawn. It pointed to Elvis' heart. At the bottom were the words, "Guess who, and where?"

The local FBI agent decided that this threat had to be taken seriously. Security was boosted at the hotel. The management even offered to let Elvis skip the show, but he wanted to go ahead with it. "I'd rather die onstage than in my bed," he said uneasily.

Between songs that night, a voice suddenly rang out. "Elvis!" a man shouted clearly. Everyone close to Elvis tensed up. Bodyguards Sonny and Red West slowly reached for their guns.

"Yeah?" Elvis shouted back. There was a moment of silence. Then the man called, "Can you sing 'Don't Be Cruel'?" Although Elvis didn't normally take requests, he was more than happy to do t**his** one!

Fortunately, nothing ever came of the threats on Elvis' life.

Elvis looks relaxed and happy at a Las Vegas press conference. Sitting next to him is his father, Vernon.

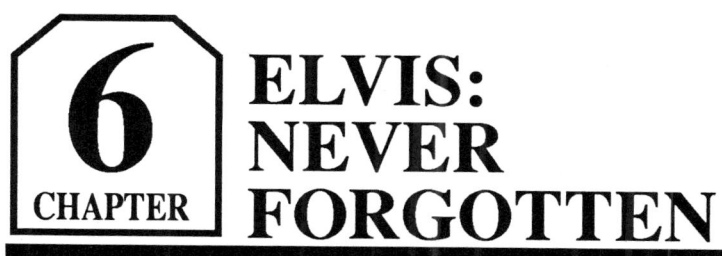

CHAPTER 6 — ELVIS: NEVER FORGOTTEN

"One night when I was about five or six, we were watching TV. I looked up at him and said, 'Daddy, Daddy, I don't want you to die.' And he just looked down at me and said 'O.K., I won't. Don't worry about it.'"

—Elvis' daughter, Lisa Marie

Up and Down

Las Vegas engagements and short concert tours now took the place of the movies and sound tracks Elvis used to do. Between tours, he scheduled in his recording sessions. No one knew what would happen at one of these sessions. Sometimes Elvis worked nonstop for days and got dozens of good songs. Other times he recorded just a few songs, or cancelled the session altogether.

Part of the problem was that Elvis often got depressed at the end of his tours. He usually slept all day and stayed up all night. He also overate, consuming bags of cheeseburgers or a quart of ice cream at a single sitting. Then he'd have to diet and work out like mad when it came time for his next tour. Eventually, of course, it all caught up with him.

Prescription drugs contributed to the problem. To lose weight quickly, Elvis took amphetamines, or "uppers." Besides making a person more active and alert, these drugs take away a person's appetite. That's why they're often called "diet pills." Elvis first used them in the army, when his sergeant gave him some to stay awake during his night watches.

For the first few years, Elvis wasn't hooked on the drugs. And no one—not even the doctors who prescribed the drugs—thought much about it. In the 1960's there wasn't nearly the emphasis on the dangers of drugs as there is today. In fact, compared to a lot of other musicians then, Elvis could have done a lot worse.

But in the 1970's, Elvis began to depend on the drugs more and more. Besides various kinds of uppers, he started to take "downers," too, so he could rest. Then, as his health began to break down, he added painkillers and sedatives to the list. Elvis Presley was caught up in the unhealthy lifestyle that would eventually kill him.

"I Don't Want You to Die!"

Everyone close to Elvis was concerned about his behavior, including his wife, Priscilla. But after a while, it became more and more difficult for Priscilla to always put his needs ahead of her own. She had her own interests, too, and wanted to get on with her life. It just didn't seem possible to do that and still remain married to Elvis Presley.

Elvis and Priscilla saw each other less and less. Finally, in early 1972, they separated. Elvis was very upset. For six months, he wouldn't let the Memphis Mafia bring their wives or girlfriends around. He didn't want to be reminded of what he had lost.

On October 9, 1973, Elvis and Priscilla were officially divorced after six years of marriage. Unlike a lot of celebrity divorces, theirs was fairly calm.

"We'd still hold hands," said Priscilla in a 1988 interview with *Life*. "Lisa never saw any major trauma between us. No yelling or arguing...We didn't hate each other, we respected each other."

Lisa Marie, who was five years old at the time of the divorce, lived with her mother. But she visited her father often, and loved spending time at Graceland. Sometimes she saw her father take pills. Although she was too young to understand what was going on, she must have sensed that something wasn't quite right.

"One night when I was about five or six, we were watching TV," 20-year-old Lisa Marie recalled in *Life* in 1988. "I looked up at him and said, 'Daddy, Daddy, I don't want you to die.' And he just looked down at me and said, 'O.K., I won't. Don't worry about it.' I said that several times when we were alone together. He probably thought I was completely crazy. But I always felt protective of him. I guess I was picking something up."

Challenges

In the meantime, Elvis Presley's amazing career went on. He won a Bing Crosby award, one of the biggest honors in the field of music. Another documentary was made, called *Elvis On Tour*. The film won a Golden Globe award. When he performed at Madison Square Garden, he broke all attendance and box-office records. Even the highway running past Graceland was renamed the Elvis Presley Boulevard in his honor.

Besides performing in concert, Elvis was also putting out a lot of albums. Although his name wasn't at the top of the charts anymore, most of his records would usually sell over a million copies.

One of the biggest challenges for Elvis—and Colonel Parker, no doubt—was the "Aloha Satellite Show" broadcast from Hawaii in January 1973. Well over one billion people would eventually see the concert. To get ready for this big event, Elvis dieted and rehearsed like never before. When showtime came, the 38-year-old performer truly looked the part of a star.

The show was more successful than even the Colonel could have predicted. When the special was broadcast in the United States in April, it easily beat out the very popular "All in the Family" television show. And in Japan, where the show was seen live, all television records were broken. Elvis got 98 percent of the viewing audience!

Among Friends

Elvis had been a worldwide sensation almost since his first songs hit the charts. Yet for some reason, he never made an overseas tour. And once the excitement of the "Aloha" special had worn off, he seemed to feel he didn't have any challenges left. Or maybe he was just tired of it all.

In any case, Elvis would never again be the dynamic performer he'd been in the past. As his weight ballooned and his pill consumption went up, his health problems kept getting worse. His heart was enlarged. His colon was twisted. His liver was damaged, and his eyes were damaged by glaucoma. Every once in a while he'd check into a hospital to "dry out," but he never managed to change his ways. He'd often have his bodyguards sneak him some cheeseburgers, and he'd usually start the pills again as soon as he got home.

Elvis did continue to do tours and Las Vegas engagements, but they sometimes had to be cancelled because of poor health. After a time, his performances suffered. The karate kicks and energetic stage moves he used to do were out of the question. His monologues often rambled on and on. And a few times he actually brought the lyric sheets to new songs on stage with him!

The critics, who just a few years ago were full of praise for Elvis, didn't hesitate to cut him down. The supermarket tabloids jumped in, too. "Elvis at 40: Paunchy, Depressed and Living in Fear" read one *National Enquirer* headline.

Despite the negative publicity, people still

turned out by the thousands to see his shows.

In December 1975, Elvis made up some of his missing engagements at the Hilton in Las Vegas. December is usually a pretty slow month in Las Vegas. Even top performers see lots of empty seats in the audience. But Elvis Presley was no ordinary star. His shows sold out, as usual. In fact, he drew in so many people that the Hilton's slot machine revenue was doubled!

Elvis' supporters knew the score. Who cared if Elvis Presley wasn't the same performer he used to be? They had gotten older, too. They knew what it was like to worry about their weight. They knew the pain of divorce. But that didn't stop them from coming to his shows and having a good time. As one writer described it, Elvis' shows were like "a visit among friends."

That visit was about to come to an end.

A World
In Shock

A lot of people had written about Elvis during his career. No one, however, had quite the same viewpoint as the authors of *Elvis: What Happened?* This book was written by his former bodyguards Sonny West, Red West, and Dave Hebler, together with Australian gossip columnist Steve Dunleavy. The book, which was released in the summer of 1977, revealed a side of Elvis that few people knew about at that time. Included in the book were stories about his drug abuse, temper, and paranoia.

Elvis was bothered by the book, naturally. But he didn't seem overly upset. He was looking forward to another tour. And nine-year-old Lisa Marie was at Graceland for a long summer visit. It was life as usual for Elvis Presley.

Then, on August 16, his body was found slumped on the bathroom floor.

At 2:33 p.m., Elvis' road manager, Joe Esposito, called for an ambulance. He said only that someone at Graceland was having trouble breathing. The ambulance crew thought a fan must have fainted outside Graceland's gates—something that happened quite often in the summer. But when the ambulance crew arrived at Graceland, they were directed to the mansion. There they found Elvis' personal doctor frantically performing CPR on his famous patient.

The doctor continued to administer CPR on the way to the hospital. "Breathe, Presley, breathe!" he shouted. But the body was already turning blue, and Elvis Presley was pronounced dead at 3:30 p.m. Within half an hour, the whole world got the news.

The official cause of death was a severely irregular heartbeat, with drugs as a contributing factor.

Almost immediately, mourners started making their way to Graceland. People came from all over the country, wanting to be near their hero one last time. In the crowd of nearly 80,000 people, strangers became friends as they cried and prayed together.

A second tragedy took place when a drunk driver plowed through the crowd, killing two girls and injuring another.

The Graceland yard was strewn with more than 2,200 flower arrangements from grieving fans. Some were in the shape of hound dogs or guitars. The florists in Memphis couldn't keep up with the demand. They had to fly in extra shipments of flowers. Later, Vernon Presley decided to give the flowers to the gathered fans as a remembrance.

After a simple funeral, the white Cadillac hearse bearing Elvis Presley's body was followed by a stately procession of 17 white Cadillac limousines. A few miles away, in the Forest Hill Cemetery, the body of Elvis Presley was laid to rest.

Today, the graves of Elvis Presley, his mother and father, and his paternal grandmother are located in the peaceful Meditation Garden at Graceland. Fans come here to dream, to pray, and most of all, to remember the singer who touched so many lives.

"I Always Felt He Was Singing To Me"

The day Elvis was buried, a memorial service was also held in Tupelo, near the two-room shack where Elvis and his twin brother were born. One of the first people to sit down in the folding chairs was a farmer's wife named Rosemary Coggins. As she spoke to a reporter from *Rolling Stone*, she—perhaps better than anyone—helped explain what Elvis Presley meant to the world.

"I was about ten years old when he hit it big," Rosemary said. "My daddy was a sharecropper and so I couldn't get an Elvis skirt and I couldn't afford to see him at the Tupelo Fair, but I always felt he was singing to **me**. ...Elvis never made me feel left out. He always made me feel like I was as pretty as Priscilla."

Then she added, "He made a lot of us feel that way."

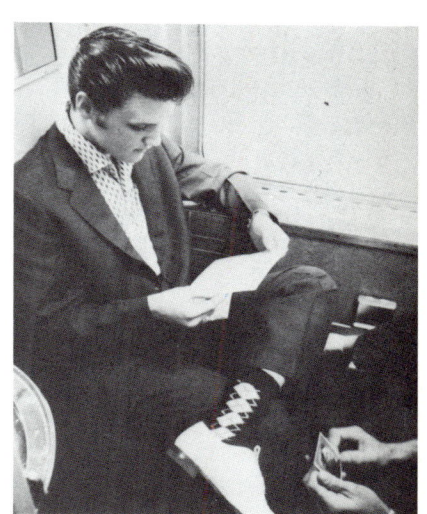

Best Wishes
Elvis Presley

GLOSSARY

accompaniment—a musical part that adds to the main part, such as playing the piano for a singer.
amphetamines—drugs that stimulate or increase the activity of the central nervous system. "Uppers."
basic training—the first period of instruction for a new military recruit.
chords—three or more notes that sound good together when played at the same time.
country music—American music that developed from the folk style of the rural South.
critic—a person who analyzes or reviews performances or works of art as a profession. Can also mean a person who is critical or negative.
deferment—an official delay of military service.
documentary—a film that presents factual information about a person or event.
drafted—to be called by the government to serve in the military.
encore—a demand by an audience for a repeat of a work.
engagement—when a performer is hired for a set period of time.
gigs—specific jobs as a musician.
glaucoma—an eye disease that causes pressure to build up within the eyeball and may lead to loss of vision.
gospel music—religious songs with a simple melody and harmony.
hepatitis—a disease that damages the liver.
karate—the Oriental art of self-defense, which makes use of special kicks and punches.

GLOSSARY

laryngitis—a condition in which the vocal cords are swollen, making speech or singing difficult.
lyric sheet—the words of a musical piece.
microphone—an electronic device that "picks up" sound.
petition—a formal, written request signed by a lot of people.
phenomenon—an out-of-the-ordinary person or event.
promotion, promotional—something used to increase publicity or sales.
psychic—supernatural powers of the mind.
rejuvenation—to make something like new again.
resurrection—to raise from the dead; revive.
rhythm & blues—black American vocal music, usually used for dancing.
rock 'n' roll—popular American music that combines aspects of country, folk and blues. It has a heavy beat and usually includes electronic instruments, such as the electric guitar.
satellite—a device in space that can be used to quickly beam television signals.
segregation—separation of people based on race, sex, age, etc; opposite of integration.
single—a record that has one short song on each side. The song that is more popular or important is usually considered the "single."
sound track—the part of a movie or show that involves music or narration
tabloid—a small newspaper with short articles and a lot of pictures.

INDEX

"Aloha Satellite Show" 6, 98-99
army 65-66, 68-69, 70, 79, 95
Beatles 47, 75, 81
Binder, Steve 84, 86
Black, Bill 30, 32, 35
Blue Moon Boys 35-36
blues music 19, 30-31, 35
country music 8, 19, 32-33, 35, 38
Crown Electric Company 26, 41
drugs, drug abuse 94-95, 97, 99, 102-103
Elvis: What Happened? 102
Graceland 10, 11, 64, 76, 83, 97-98, 102-104
"Grand Ole Opry" 33-34
Hawaii 6, 73, 98
Hilton International Hotel 87, 89, 101
Hume High School 20, 23, 85
Keisker, Marion 28-30
"Louisiana Hayride" 33-36
Memphis Mafia 76-78, 83, 96
Moore, Scotty 30, 32, 35
movies 51-52, 65-66, 70, 73, 79-81, 84

Neal, Bob 35-36, 39
Parker, Colonel Tom 38-40, 43-44, 47, 50-51, 79-80, 87, 98
Pearl, Minnie 73-74
Phillips, Dewey 31
Phillips, Sam 27-31, 33, 40
Presley, Dee 72
Presley, Gladys 14-19, 21, 26, 40, 42, 67, 104
Presley, Jesse Garon 15
Presley, Lisa Marie 10, 83, 93, 97, 102
Presley, Priscilla (Beaulieu) 10, 69, 72, 82-83, 96-97, 105
Presley, Vernon 14, 18, 21, 40, 67, 72, 82, 104
RCA/Victor 40, 44, 48, 86
Starlight Wranglers 32
Sullivan, Ed 42, 47-48
Sun Records 27, 30, 32, 35, 40
television appearances 43-47, 70, 84-86
Tupelo, Mississippi 9, 14, 105
West, Red 23, 91, 102
West, Sonny 91, 102

LISTENING CHOICES

Songs

"Are You Lonesome Tonight"
"Blue Suede Shoes"
"Don't Be Cruel"
"Good Rockin' Tonight"
"Heartbreak Hotel"
"Hound Dog"
"I Can't Help Falling
    in Love With You"
"If I Can Dream"
"Jailhouse Rock"
"Love Me Tender"
"Mystery Train"
"Peace in the Valley"
"Shake, Rattle and Roll"
"Suspicious Minds"
"Teddy Bear"
"That's All Right, Mama"

Albums

A Date with Elvis
Blue Hawaii
Elvis is Back
From Elvis in Memphis
His Hand in Mine
How Great Thou Art
Memphis/Vegas
Moody Blues
Peace in the Valley

Movies

Love Me Tender
Loving You
Jailhouse Rock
King Creole
G.I. Blues
Flaming Star
Blue Hawaii
Girls! Girls! Girls!
*It Happened at the
    World's Fair*
Fun in Acapulco
Kissin' Cousins
Viva Las Vegas
Roustabout
Paradise, Hawaiian Style
Easy Come, Easy Go
Clambake
Speedway
Live a Little, Love a Little
Charro
The Trouble with Girls
Change of Habit
Elvis: That's the Way It Is
    (documentary)
Elvis On Tour (documentary)

MAR 07 1990

CHILDREN'S ROOM
METUCHEN PUBLIC LIBRARY